Enhancing YOUR LIFE *One Strand at a Time*

THE NEXT CHAPTER

Written by
Nekesa Namosuge J. Smith

For permission requests, contact Nekesa Smith at officialnekesa@gmail.com. Silver Bangles Productions books may be purchased for educational, business, or sales promotional use at www.silverbanglesproductions.com. For more information, please email info@silverbanglesproductions.com.
Book Cover Design: Beautifully Driven Media
Cover Photo: Beautifully Driven Media
Content Photography: Istanbul, Turkey
Cover Hair: NNR Studio & Academy
Printed in Atlanta, GA, U.S.A.
First printing, March 2026
Library of Congress Control Number: 2026907250
ISBN: 978-1-972235-00-3

This book is dedicated to James D. Johnson and Ida M. Johnson for being the best parents a girl could ask for. Thank you for always being there for me and providing the necessary tools needed for me to walk into my dreams. Thank you Dad for building out every salon I owned, and Mom for your unwavering support. I love you both.

-Nekesa

FOREWORD

I have known Nekesa Smith for many years and have watched her move through rooms with quiet authority - hands steady, voice calm, presence grounded. I have also watched women sit in her chair carrying more than tangled strands. Without words, you can tell that many of these women carried doubt, were overworked and overburdened, filled with questions about who they were allowed to be.

Enhancing Your Life One Strand at a Time: The Next Chapter enters a cultural conversation that is long overdue. Hair has always been more than style for Black women. Black women's hair has signaled identity, resistance, assimilation, artistry, and survival, and speaks volumes, shaping how others read us before we even speak.

In hip hop culture, you could often identify the era by the way women MCs wore their hair. With over 50 years of hip-hop, styles have changed, shifting from braids, fades, curls, to wraps. Each style spoke to social climate, politics, confidence, and creative ownership. Hair became archive. It recorded struggle and triumph without spitting a single lyric.

Black women have endured discrimination tied to natural and textured styles. We know hair bias exists in workplaces, classrooms, and even within our own communities. Policies have attempted to regulate what grows from our scalps. Comments have long policed what is deemed professional or acceptable. The impact is not cosmetic, but psychological, and it's institutionally supported.

As an educator and consultant who has worked with schools across the United States and internationally, I have seen how feelings about beauty shape performance. When a woman feels affirmed in her identity, her leadership strengthens. When she feels pressured to conform, energy diverts from innovation to survival. If a woman questions whether she belongs, whether she looks right, or whether she is enough, that internal conflict follows her into every boardroom, classroom, and leadership space, negatively impacting her performance.

During my years as a school leader in the Middle East, I served alongside Black women from across the diaspora. African American. Ethiopian. Somalian. South African. Each carried her own hair story into a desert climate that was unforgiving to textured strands. Nekesa stepped into that environment with expertise and care. She restored moisture, style, and more importantly, confidence. Women left her chair standing taller.

That is what makes this memoir credible. Nekesa writes from lived experience and professional practice. She understands technique, texture, and what it means to choose yourself again after years of shrinking.

This book matters because it refuses to treat beauty as trivial. It frames it as a journey. There are potholes, peaks, and valleys. There are seasons of concealment and seasons of bold display. The journey of beauty mirrors the journey of many women in hip hop culture. You claim your voice, but first, you must *define* it.

As you read these pages, consider what strands you have carried too long. Notice what parts of yourself are ready for renewal. This is more than a beauty memoir. It is a call to stand firmly in your texture, your story, and your purpose.

I recommend this book to every woman who needs the reminder that you are worthy of care, visibility, and walking boldly in who you are.

-Dr. Crystal LaVoulle

Founder | The LaVoulle Group, International Education Consultants

TABLE OF CONTENTS

Spelman College
Bachelor of Arts
CAIRO
BEIJING
PARIS
SYDNEY
BERLIN
LISBON
MADRID
RIO DE JANEIRO
LONDON
DELHI
HONG KONG
STOCKHOLM
NEKESA'S
NATURAL
Radiance
NEKESA J.SMITH,BA,MC

DEAR READER

Hey Radiant Beauty,

Is your hair naturally textured, coily, or kinky? Do you find yourself getting frustrated or overwhelmed when trying to style your hair? Have you been looking for a little bit of hair inspiration and insider secrets to start or *continue* the journey towards loving and rocking your natural hair? If you answered yes to any of those questions, keep reading.

The struggle of figuring out how and what to do with our hair texture has proven itself to be its own unique challenge. There are tons of products available with minimal education on how to actually use them, specifically for our hair texture. Many of us have never even seen our own natural curl pattern, whether that's tightly coiled tresses or loose curls. And some of us have no idea how to properly take care of the crown that sits upon our heads.

So what do we do?

I wrote this book to be both a memoir and a how-to, beauty empowerment guide, where you will learn everything from how to define your hair texture and styles to explore, to how to be empowered and naturally radiant. There is a void of beauty empowerment. Media and society constantly tells us how we *should* look and what our hair *should* look like. This book is here to help fill the needs of girls and women all around the world. Those of us who want to own our natural, radiant beauty. Whether your hair is kinky, curly, coily, or wavy, this book was written for you.

So to answer the question, *what do we do?*, well, we turn the page, and start the journey.

Xo, Nekesa

THE MAKING OF A RADIANT HAIR GODDESS

Growing up with a name like Nekesa, I was sure that I was born to be extraordinary. As a child, I was a creative spirit with my own style. My family was used to seeing me adorned in outfits my mother had not picked out. She once told me that when I was three, I would change outfits four or five times a day. According to her, I would even come out of my room from playing, with different hairstyles she did not create.

By the age of five I had become obsessed with hair. I can clearly remember cutting and braiding my Barbie doll's hair with hundreds of small braids, regularly. I once had a doll with yarn hair that would lengthen to indicate her hair was growing. That was the coolest thing to me. I loved watching her hair grow mechanically. Well one day, I wanted to try something on my own hair. I was a little bit older, around eight years old, when I got the idea to cut the yarn out of the doll's hair and braid it into my own hair. I couldn't believe it worked. I thought it looked perfect! I was so excited I had successfully executed what I thought was a great idea. Well, my mother, on the other hand, did not. When she saw me, she was completely shocked. Luckily for me, she was busy getting ready for her doctor's appointment, so she could not do anything in the moment. She simply gave me one of those, "*We will deal with this later,*" looks that moms give, and we were out the door.

Thirty minutes later, there we were in the waiting room at the doctor's office in the middle of the day in New Haven, Connecticut, and I'm sitting there with yarn braided into my hair. That experience was my display of exploration and innovation. Looking back at that moment, it was the beginning of my journey to becoming a beauty inventor of braids and twist extension methods. It was the beginning of Nekesa's Natural Radiance (NNR) Serenity Twist.

In addition to styling my own hair, along with the heads of my Barbie dolls, I also dabbled in product creation. I would stand at the kitchen counter for hours, blending different ingredients, seeing what worked well together, seeing what smelled nice, noting what didn't. I had eczema and would study botany and the science of natural ingredients, like oatmeal, honey, and aloe vera, in an effort to soothe my eczema. I would use mayonnaise and eggs to create treatments that added shine and strength to hair. I was always curious about the ingredients of hair and skin products, looking for ways to improve manageability. Once I read Madame C.J. Walker's story, I was activated.

Another thing I loved to do was getting up early Saturday morning to tag along with my Mom to go to the Beauty Shop. Mom's beautician, Ms. Viola, was the owner of a three-chair salon. Her salon was always full, there would either be women under dryers, in salon chairs, or sitting in a waiting chair, where I usually was. In the waiting area, there would be women patiently waiting for their glamor moment. Usually these women were walk-ins, sometimes waiting for an hour or more because Ms. Viola's appointment book stayed full.

Joining my mom on her biweekly hair appointments was such a treat for me. While some kids might dread these trips and impatiently count down the minutes till they could leave, I thoroughly enjoyed being at the hair salon. I loved hearing the stories of the women in the beauty shop. While many of these stories contained serious topics that the women were navigating, they always seemed to have a comedic twist that didn't negate the intention of the story. I enjoyed everything about the salon, from the different hairstyles I saw to the smell of Dax pressing oil.

The conversations that clients shared with each other created a strong sense of community. Their honesty, bluntness, and ability to be unashamedly candid back then in the 80s, were similar to how modern day bloggers and vloggers are today. It was always special to see how the women transformed when Ms. Viola handed them the handheld mirror to see the finished look. During that moment you could see that the women focused fully on themselves. Just for a second, their day-to-day worries and concerns seemed to vanish. Although it could have been a simple shampoo and set, to them it brought sheer joy. Their personal standard of beauty was renewed and revived, and the feeling that brings, is indescribable.

My Grandmother Nancy Davis Walker birthed eight daughters, so I had a host of cousins. Our birthday parties consisted of *all cousins*. We were so close that sometimes my cousins felt more like sisters and brothers. For a while, each cousin had a birthday year twin. Coming from a large family, it seemed as if we were always attending some kind of family function. After relatives got wind of my talent, I started braiding my cousins' hair at almost every family gathering I attended. Eventually, I started making tip money from aunts who requested that I do their daughter's hair. Doing this, was like running my own business. In addition to my allowance, I had created another source of income from simply doing something I loved. I did this for a few years. Arriving to family functions with my family in the afternoon. Speaking to and laughing with family members, grabbing a plate of some good food, and then getting to work. Literally. Sometimes I would do multiple cousins' heads at one family event, not finishing until well into the night.

It wasn't until I was 12 years old that I started becoming popular for my skills in hair. I had started taking clients at my parents' house like it was a salon. I set a special chair for hair next to a table where I placed all my hair tools. On my styling table were combs, brushes, a blow dryer, and Conair plug-in curling irons. My set up was comfortable. I was easily making money by doing something I loved and bringing joy to the people I styled. From that point on, all I did was dream about having my own business as a real salon owner.

MY MENTOR MOMENT

My first encounter with a mentor was my mother. I remember spending hours looking through her closet, admiring her shoes, jewelry, and bags. My mother is and has always been a stylish woman. Not flashy, but intentional in how she chose to present herself. She liked to wear her hair a certain way and loved for everything to look sophisticated and put together. She carried this same approach to other aspects in her life as well. Everything from her home, car, wardrobe, to even her children's dental care, was intentionally curated and crafted.

I always knew that I was supposed to learn from my mother. She would often call me into the kitchen when she was cooking so that I could watch and learn. At the time I was not into the idea of cooking, I much rathered being in the kitchen to build a beauty business.

My mother mentored me into becoming a great hairstylist by allowing me to practice on her hair. She encouraged me to pursue my passion without doubting me or trying to hold me back from my dreams, despite the fact that they may not have been aligned with hers or what hers were for me.

By the time I was 14 years old, I went from styling my family's hair to styling the heads of my classmates and the hair of their mothers. It amazed me how many people trusted me to do their hair, especially at such a young age. At this point in my life, my only form of training was the Dudley brochures that I owned, along with a monthly subscription to hair magazines. Dudley Cosmetology University was an advanced education and training institution founded by Dr. Joe and Eunice Dudley in North Carolina in 1968. Their mission was to elevate the Black Beauty Industry, which was and is something I've always been passionate about.

I remember doing my first sew-in. My mother was preparing for a trip to New York. She had spent over $500 on a hair weave and this was in 1984, so this trip was clearly a big deal. She wore the hair weave for a while, and then when she was ready to change styles, I took her hair out. From there, I was able to teach myself how to do sew-ins by removing the hair from the sew-in, studying her stylist's technique, and then re-sewing it in. Nowadays, that is known as an installation, but back then, it was simply called, a hair weave. That was my mother's first hair weave and the last one she received from another stylist. After that, I became my mother's primary stylist.

My second encounter with a mentor was when I was around the age of 14. Her name was Mrs. N'Naomi Knox. Mrs. Knox was the first person, outside of my mother, who really took me under her wing. She invested her time and resources into me and introduced me to things she felt I should know - *nuggets of wisdom* I call them - to be successful in the hair business. Mrs. Knox believed in my skill set and allowed me to style and maintain her daughter's hair for years. They both became great friends of mine, trusting my expertise in style options and hair care. Mrs. Knox assisted with shaping the foundation for my business. She introduced me to different products, people, and experiences. She was very instrumental in many of my endeavors, including helping me become a debutante in 1990.

When I look back at the history of the Knox's and I, I see the true importance of a mentor. A mentor can be a person of inspiration because of their story and journey. You can use that inspiration to achieve your own goals. And that's exactly what my mother and Mrs. Knox helped me to do. A mentor can also be someone you never met, a mental mentor. Madame C.J. Walker and the Dudleys were my mental mentors. I never met either, however I studied and implemented tools and practices from them all.

Nekesa's Tips

Having a mentor is an excellent element in your career. A mentor can not walk your journey for you nor can they guarantee that you won't have any hiccups along the road. You may stumble and even fall, but a good mentor will always be there to offer a helping hand, love, and advice on how to get back on your grind. Mentors help prevent any major issues from breaking you; advising you based on their experiences.

My advise?

- Find a mentor from your school, church, or organization you're a part of. Spaces that you already frequent are the best places to seek a mentor because it is familiar to both you and the mentor.
- Set a meeting with your potential mentor by email, phone, or through a letter. The way you approach your future mentor is very important because it is your introduction. It sets the foundation of communication. It says who you are, what you are looking to do. It brings clarity to the mentor of exactly how they can help you.
- Keep a journal so when you meet with a mentor, you have an ample amount of questions and you are able to have direct conversations about what you are seeking.
- Stay in contact with your mentor quarterly to touch bases on progress, ask questions and discuss forward intentions.
- Become a mentor yourself; remember to see the change you would like to see, you must first, become it.

THE CROWN IS YOURS, WEAR IT

When I was 16, my parents decided to move to California. Up until that point I had spent my whole life in New Haven, Connecticut. I was doing well in school, was surrounded by lots of family and friends, and on top of that, I had clients. I was not thrilled about moving across the country. Naturally, I was very reluctant. I was a teenager from New Haven, and although we were not too far from the city, my life seemed to revolve around the areas I was used to. I felt as if there was no other city as great as my small town.

Once we moved to Sacramento, it was not hard for me to stand out and for people to notice my artistic flair. I had style and my hair was always fly. It didn't take long for me to start doing hair again. Soon enough, I had created the salon atmosphere in my parents' new Californian home. Since I had over the amount of credits needed to graduate from a California high school, I had the option of going to cosmetology school during the day. So I went to high school from 8am - 10am and cosmetology school from 11am - 5pm. That is where my life as a career driven cosmetologist began.

There, I met two of my great friends from the west coast that I'm still connected to, Anitra and Tavia. Anitra realized that she was not passionate about working in hair, so she went on to become an attorney. Tavia is now a successful hair stylist and salon owner. She, like me, was so excited about hair. I had finally met someone who shared the same zest for hair as me, she actually may have actually loved it more than me! We hit if off from the start; all we did was have fun and talk about hair.

While I was offered several opportunities in California, I was never truly a California girl. My friends and the fly style of Connecticut were calling. So after only a year, I answered and moved back at the age of 17.

Once I went back home to New Haven, I was welcomed with such warm embrace. I was excited because here I was, back in Connecticut, my old stomping grounds, and it was on. I had graduated from both high school and completed some of cosmetology school, and my skills were getting better every day. The idea now, was that I would go to nursing school and do hair on the side. My high-school in Connecticut was a health and business magnet school. I chose to study science and thought I wanted to become a nurse. New Haven, Connecticut is home to Yale University and Hospital, so the medical industry was a strong career choice in Connecticut.

After enrolling in some classes, I quickly knew that the medical field was not the route I wanted to take. So I had to figure something else out. I had spent the last twelve years of my life being a student, so now I was ready to get serious about making some money. The problem though, was that I had no car, no apartment, and no job. In fact, I was living at my grandmother's house. It wasn't at all what I had planned, but it ended up working out for the best. I've always been a pretty independent person, so while I lived with my grandma, I offered to give her some money to help with extra expenses. I wanted to contribute and prove that I was responsible. As long as I checked in with her and let her know if I was staying out, she was fine and allowed me the freedom to do what I pleased.

Living with my grandma and paying what I could was my current living situation, but there was still the issue of the fact that I needed a job. I didn't have a car, so I relied on friends or public transportation to get around. But despite being young, I wasn't trying to hang out all around town. I knew that there was only *one* location I had to be at in order to be successful, and that was Tanika's Beauty Salon on Whalley Avenue.

Shortly after moving back to Connecticut to live with my grandmother, I saw an advertisement from Tanika's saying that they were hiring for licensed stylists. At the time, I had around 300 of the 1500 hours required to take the state board exam and become a licensed cosmetologist. I was only a fifth of the way there. However, one of the lessons I learned from my parents growing up was to work hard for what you want and to never take *no* for an answer. I knew that while I may not have had the license or the hours, I had the skills to pay the bills.

After a few days of contemplating, I decided that I wanted the job and I was willing to work hard for it. The next morning, I walked into Tanika's and inquired about the position. There were three stylists there at the time, Mark, Tina, and Jamaican Jenny, who eventually bought and took over the salon. There was only one girl there around my age, Sherell, who went by Rell. I inquired and applied for the position all at once. I was confident and a strong communicator, so before the owner, Mr. Edwards, even asked, I had already explained that I had just moved back from California and that I would love to bring in some models during my interview to showcase my work. He agreed. By the next day, I had gathered my friends together and did their complete hair styling in the salon. Mr. Edwards knew that I didn't have a license, so he offered me a base salary of $250.00 a week, with an option to make more if I rented a booth. Back in 1993, $250.00 a week was great, because I had no financial responsibilities. I accepted the offer and was there the next day with my tools and equipment, ready to work.

Some months had passed and I was still pleased with my new position. I was good at what I did and I did it all, from relaxers, short cuts, and ponytails to finger waves and scrunchies by the ton. For me, an average Friday consisted of about 35 - 40 customers, and then I would wake up to do the same thing the next morning. My weekends were busy and my schedule was full. Things were going well. I was handling the regulars at the salon and helping bring in new clients as well. So I decided to meet with Mr. Edwards. I negotiated some additional marketing, and began making $1000.00 a week. At the age of 18, I was balling! Making that kind of money with little to no financial obligations turned me into a shopaholic. I would take the train to the city and shop until I dropped!

In a small town like New Haven, news gets around fast, and sometimes that caused issues to quickly arise. A lot started happening that made me put my current situation into perspective. I was making great money, however, I still had no car and I was not enrolled in school. And in my personal life, it was like I was in a loop. I needed a change. One piece of advice that I vividly recall my co-worker giving me is, "Nay-Nay, you are respected like a professional. You need to start addressing your customers as clientele and get more serious." It took me a while, but eventually that's what I did.

I began to take my work and myself a lot more seriously. I realized that faith and action is the formula towards confidence and positive outcomes. The crown is yours, you truly just have to make the decision to wear it.

Nekesa's Tips

Becoming a true beauty professional takes time, charisma, and consistency.

- Always take time to enhance yourself through reading, taking classes, and constantly thinking outside the box.
- Stay in the spirit of gratitude for your God given gift and all the fruits of your labor.
- Stay patient when building your clientele. Being anxious during the client building process can take you off track and make you unfocused.
- Always carry business cards with you and don't be afraid to pass them out. Face-to-face consultation helps the potential client get comfortable with you.
- Always wear your hair in a head-turning style; make sure your hair and your choice of clothing is unique, but classy.

BEAUTIFULLY DRIVEN TO THE HAIR CAPITAL

The Bronner Brothers show is a well-known, worldwide hair show that you *have* to experience if you are in the hair industry. It's held in Atlanta, Georgia, which is an 18-hour drive from Connecticut. It was 1993 and Sherell from the shop, three of my friends, and I decided that we *had* to go to the hair show. We piled in a small rental car and headed to Atlanta.

The drive alone was something else, but we made it! The whole trip was sketchy from the car to the hotel. Coming from Connecticut to Atlanta was a complete culture shock. We tripped off the guys wearing finger waves and relaxers. We laughed about the southern drawl and the style of clothing. We truly had a ball!

The hair show was a life-changing experience for me. It was like going to the World Series, but for hair. I was blessed to meet many all-star hairstylists, such as Charles Gregory and Barry Fletcher. I was exposed to many new styling techniques and looks. I even saw new ways to do the styles I had already mastered. It was an incredible opportunity to just be in the same room with so many icons in the hair industry, and to have a front row seat in watching them work was amazing. As my time in Atlanta dwindled down, I knew that this would not be my last appearance in the Dirty South. I began dreaming of myself styling on that very stage at the Bronner Brothers Hair Show.

Although my friends and I had only been in Atlanta for a few days, and the majority of our time was spent inside a convention center, I noticed a number of differences between Atlanta and Connecticut. For instance, the surge of entrepreneurship, positive

Blackness, culture, and the sun, which was a huge plus because I'd absolutely had it with the snow. I had grown up with it my whole life and the one year I had spent in Sacramento, showed just how sweet, and *warm*, the other side can be. I was ready to play and slay in the Atlanta sun. I knew that I had to come back.

After an inspiring trip to Atlanta that left me looking forward to my next visit, I was quickly greeted with the reality of nonsense there was to deal with upon my return to New Haven. One day I was working on a client and chatting with my friend in the salon when the phone rang. Within ten minutes, a car full of girls came racing into the salon screaming and trying to fight. The next thing I knew, they were macing the salon. Unfazed by the mace, I left my client and ran after the girls. I couldn't believe what had just happened. I felt so disrespected that I wasn't even thinking straight. I literally ran out of the salon by myself into the lair of those girls. I later found out that all the fuss was because there was an issue between four of the girls, and they chose to carry our their problem at the salon. Unfortunately this would not be the last time I witnessed or was thrown into the midst of some foolishness at my job. I tried to deal with it as best as I could for as long as I could, but it wasn't long before my family started to hear about some of the salon shenanigans I had to endure, and was not pleased.

After that incident, I started reflecting on my time in New Haven and thinking seriously about my future. It seemed as if everyone around me was content with having a good job with benefits, a cute apartment, and a car. But even back then, I knew I wanted more than that. I wanted to live a certain lifestyle and it did not include the foolishness I was dealing with in New Haven. After a while, I began to feel like I was running out of time. That season of my life felt difficult and awkward; it was the feeling of things coming to an end.

One evening, we were all finishing up in the salon. Mr. Edwards usually locked the door at sunset, but on this particular day, he forgot. The front of the salon was all windows, so we could see whatever was going on outside. That night, we saw a guy walking fast, quickly approaching the salon. It looked odd, but we didn't want to jump to conclusions. Well, he walked in. The first reaction came from Mark, who screamed. When I looked up, I saw the guy pointing a nine-millimeter gun in the direction of all of the stylists, demanding all of our money. I was so nervous, I had no idea what to do. It didn't help that some close friends of mine had been killed recently by gun violence. I opened my salon station drawer that was full of cash, then ran to the back along with the rest of the staff. Mr. Edwards, who had seen and done it all in his life, calmly sat in his same seat and slowly gave the man some money. Well, Mr. Edwards might have been calm, but I was not. That was strike two, and that incident offered me a well-needed touch of reality. New Haven was getting more and more dangerous, and I was quickly outgrowing it.

When I thought about my life in New Haven, nothing seemed promising. Although I was making great money, I constantly found myself making bad choices and ending up in the same place over and over again. So what could I do? I knew that I didn't want to be in Connecticut anymore, but I also knew I didn't want to live in California. I had no plans for moving and felt I was not yet in a position to do so anyway. So I stayed, and kept working.

A few months later, the girls and I were finishing up a long day at the salon. There was a Chinese take-out restaurant right next door, so I decided to get something to eat before heading out for the night. As I exited the door, I walked maybe two feet towards the Chinese restaurant when I heard someone call my name. This wasn't unusual, since the salon was around the corner from my house, a lot of people knew me. When I turned around to see who called my name, I saw a girl swinging a hammer at me. It all happened so fast. The next thing I knew, I was waking up on the middle of the sidewalk and everyone was out of the salon, crowding around me, asking if I was alright. Someone called my family and 911, and I was escorted back into the salon. I remember looking in the mirror and seeing blood gush from my head from where that girl grazed the side of my head with a hammer. Heated, with blood still flowing from my head, I ran outside to try to find the girl, because at this point, I still didn't know who she was or why she attacked me with a hammer. When I went outside, I saw my aunt rocking a car. The girl was inside, hiding, and my aunt was trying to get her out. By the time the ambulance finally arrived and I got to the hospital, my parents had been notified about what happened, and they were outraged.

With that incident, I saw my life flash before my eyes. It was then that I knew that I needed to make a life-changing decision. While I was furious at the girl for attacking me, I knew it would do me no good to find her and ask questions. There was no need for me to get revenge. This was strike three. It was time for me to leave New Haven.

Nekesa's Tips

- Decide what makes you happy and then work towards developing your craft.
- Never think of the monetary reward; give your all to whatever you want to do as if you are getting paid. This will eventually lead to funds coming in.
- Always remember that what you put in is exactly what you get out; put your all into your work to receive an abundance of what you are seeking.
- Have faith in all things and apply actions behind that faith.
- Never stop learning; always have a teachable spirit.
- Know when it's time to go. There is no shame in moving on.

THE DECISION TO WEAR MY CROWN

I was a Catholic student for years before begging my parents to go to a public school. While I was a member of a popular Baptist church where I sang in the choir, I would also sometimes attend a Pentecostal church with my grandmother. I even did community service at a young age. My faith and my relationship with God was deep and clear. But nothing would compare to the connection I had begun to develop with God during *this* time in my life. My family, friends, and I were all angry with the girl, but for me, the anger did not last long. It did not take me long to forgive and release all negative feelings I had towards her. I knew that there was no changing what happened. I was blessed to be healthy and in my right mind because she obviously was not. I knew that by forgiving her and moving on from all of the drama, I would open myself to infinite possibilities of the future, and a new life in Atlanta.

Finally, my decision was made. I found a private cosmetology school called Osborne School of Cosmetology, which was run by Mrs. O. It was located in Atlanta, and my good friend Tavia, from Sacramento, was already attending, so I was very excited to join her. Tavia had given me the information to a dorm that accepted students from the Atlanta University Center (AUC) as well as other colleges and universities. I was enrolled in school and had my dorm set. With all the drama I had been through and the money I had spent, after paying tuition for my school and my dorm fees, I left for Atlanta with $100.00 total. Now most people would never even think of moving across the country with only $100. Some would say that I was crazy to have made a move under such financial circumstances; however, at that point I was committed to God's plan and promise to me. I applied the faith of a mustard seed along with action.

My decision to wear my crown came in 1995. I was a new resident in Atlanta and enrolled in the Osborne School of Cosmetology. I was extremely eager to be the best professional hair stylist. I practiced my craft whenever I could. The commitment I had was like no other; it was almost as if I were married to the hair industry. As I started building relationships with my clients, I realized that most of them weren't truly living because of their hair. Many clients expressed to me that they had not learned how to swim and that they would go to a beach and not fully submerge themselves in the water because of their hair. This, I thought, was no way to live life. I saw this as a challenge and began searching for a solution for these ladies. I began not only studying the client's hair, but also the physiology behind their hair. I noted lifestyles, hair, and career choices, as well as how they *felt* about their natural hair texture. I learned that their workouts were limited to certain days based on when they got their hair done. There were other things that both my clients and I experienced. For example, I was wary of not wearing a scarf nightly and not being able to walk in the rain without worry. I had a shortcut and was tired of having to waste 45 minutes styling and curling my hair every day. Those were 45 minutes I could've spent reading, doing yoga, or just preparing for the day. I knew that I wanted to make a change.

My decision to go (back) natural was confirmed when I walked through the doors of Khamit Kinks natural hair salon. I was visiting New York to see a friend for a few months. This salon wasn't just any salon. To everyone who entered, it was an experience like no other. It was beautiful to be in an environment that appreciated natural hair textures. There were so many options for hair care and hair styling there.

Ruth, the owner, offered me a training internship. For me, this was an "enhance your life" moment. I enjoyed the decorative reflections of African ancestral images, artifacts, and furniture. Every hairstylist has a vision of seeing their work published in a magazine, on television, or in a movie. During my time at Khamit Kinks, I had the honor of assisting the styling of some amazing women, like Oprah Winfrey, Angela Bassett, and Terry McMillan. These women all rocked their own natural hair texture, free of chemicals. Being exposed to these powerful, beautiful, and famous women during that time in my life was pivotal and gave me the encouragement to not only wear my own hair naturally, but to also educate clients, family, and friends about this health option.

When I finally made the choice to wear my own natural hair texture, it was an amazing and liberating feeling. I enjoyed feeling my own textured coils and exploring various style options. I wore everything from extensions, silk presses, braids, twists, and an occasional curly afro, but my favorite style was a coil set. I was most satisfied with the fact that, with my hair being natural, whatever my style option was, my hair was healthy.

The decision to wear my natural hair opened me up to choosing a new lifestyle and mindset. I began traveling and enjoying a healthy lifestyle of exercising, being free, and naturally radiant. The most empowering thing that I feel a woman can do is wear her own hair. She is then able to live her life fully and embrace it. As a licensed cosmetologist, I am all for enhanced beauty, however at some point, you have to accept and love what God has given to you.

"Your crown has been paid for; you just have to wear it."
- Oprah Winfrey

Nekesa's Tips

- I make the choice to be happy.
- Today, I am enough.
- Today I will give the love I want to receive.
- I am perfectly made. My hair is perfect;
  God made my skin, hair, and nails like this.
- Know that there were no mistakes in your creation.

THE DECISION TO WEAR MY CROWN

Hair is both an expression of one's feelings and emotions. It's a reflection of one's inner beauty. When people meet you for the first time, they look at your face, hair, clothes, and shoes. That reality may be perceived as judgmental; however, that is your only form of communicating who you are when meeting someone for the first time, before words are ever exchanged. Although these are generally the facts, it doesn't make it an easy pill to swallow or even the right thing to do. But, it's the world we live in.

I have learned not to be overly concerned with what people think of me, and I encourage you to do the same. With that being said, I'm not suggesting you disregard your appearance. It's never wise to move through life looking like you don't care, especially when you're stepping into new opportunities. Your hair should be neat and intentional, because it reflects your preparation and your respect for the opportunity before you.

What has always amazed me, though, is how many women have sat in my chair and shared that they wanted to go natural, yet felt a natural 'do wasn't appropriate for a professional corporate environment. That idea has always baffled me. When I travel, my hair is embraced by everyone, professionals and nonprofessionals alike. I truly believe your inner beauty and confidence carry whatever textured hairstyle you choose. No matter what anyone else says or thinks.

When you come to a hair salon, it is a visit of necessity. Simply put, you either need your hair maintained, you need those tresses to be pampered, or you just need some well-deserved me-time.

The average salon visit takes anywhere between two to three hours. And from the time you walk into the salon, it's all about you. First, your hair is shampooed and conditioned, and depending on the condition of your hair, you may need a specialty treatment, like a protein or fortifying condtioner. While you're either sitting under the dryer or getting your hair blow-dryed, you can then look through an array of magazines the salon offers, or on your cell phone, to choose your hairspiration for what you want to have done for that particular visit. Your salon service should be one that is relaxing yet energizing. Once the stylist is done with your hair and hands you the mirror to show you his or her work, your face should be filled with bliss. I use the word "bliss" here because your hair is not only properly cleansed and treated, your hair is now polished, pampered, and ready for whatever your week has to offer. The experience is a renewal process that just feels good from then inside out.

Nowadays, everyone is wondering whether to wear their hair natural, relaxed, weaved, or pressed. The first step to becoming a hair goddess is to know that the hairstyle you're wearing is not a definition of who you are as a woman. It is merely a tiny part of you. India Aire was on to something when she said, "I am not my hair." The ideology of a hairstyle choice is for it to be something that works with your lifestyle. If you are a student, mother, teacher, doctor, athlete, or hairstylist, your career is a major part of your lifestyle and the time that you spend on doing your hair should be a factor in your schedule. That's why I say pick your hair based on your lifestyle. I suggest that my clients ask themselves these questions when choosing a style:

How much time do I have to dedicate to my hair in the morning, daily, and even on vacation?

Besides making yourself feel like a beautiful hair goddess, what else can you be spending your time on? Maybe there's a business or personal relationship you could be focusing on strengthening. Prioritize what's important in your life.

How often am I prepared to visit the salon?

Am I a weekly, monthly, or an every-season client? Define the style options and break down how long they take to do and how long they last in your hair.

Am I active? (If so) How often am I working out?

A hair goddess is a healthy, fit woman, constantly working toward better practice. She is not overly zealous about her weight, as she is on an ongoing treadmill towards great energy and health.

Am I concerned with the long-term health of my hair, skin, and body? Or do I just want a hairstyle?

Talk with your stylist about the scalp and skin disorders associated with chemicals used in relaxers. Think about the time and money spent on hair that can be spent on travel, taking on a new hobby, or doing something spontaneously adventurous. A true hair goddess has learned to let go of her hair hang-ups and chooses to live her life to the fullest.

And finally, I lovingly tell my clients to get their stuff together, because "there is a little hair-goddess-in-training looking at you." It is powerful to be proud of who you are while also believing that each generation can grow stronger than the last. Girls may love glam, and that's perfectly fine, but their minds should also be centered on believing, achieving, conceiving, and sustaining the greatness of a full life. They should never feel pressured to fit into the narrow "beauty standards" projected in the media. Those standards often limit creativity, restrict prosperity, and distract from true happiness.

10 STEPS TO LOVING YOURSELF THROUGH YOUR HAIR

1. Treat your hair as if it is your crown.

2. Your skin is your largest organ and your scalp is an extension of that. Scalp care is essential for the health and growth of your hair.

3. Use options like braids, twists, and protective styled extensions to explore what works for you.

4. Find a professional and skilled stylist to teach you while taking care of your hair.

5. Consult with a professional to find products that work for your scalp and hair texture.

6. Enhance your look every season (color, texture, style, length).

7. Wear your hair like you wear your favorite shoes, with confidence and flair.

8. Make every occasion special by expressing through your hairstyle, remember it is your crown.

9. Keep it classy and chic.

10. Love your natural texture and take care of it like the gift it is.

HOW YOU DO ONE THING IS HOW YOU DO ALL THINGS

The first salon that I worked at in Atlanta as a stylist was Phawless Hair Designs, owned by Stephanie Kennedy and her family. We were the PhDs of hair. The owners were from Southern California, Compton to be exact. I loved working there; I thought their salon was the best thing going. It was my first salon in which we had an actual fulltime receptionist. The salon also had licensed shampoo assistants, which made hairstyling easier and fun. It was the type of environment where a lot of Black doctors, teachers, dentists, and other professionals came to get their hair done. The ambiance was really nice. The salon was a 12-chair salon with a full nail care area and barbershop on the other side. The color decor was a classic black, white, and silver. The walls were full of mirrors and the floors shone equally to them. The reception area was separate from the actual clinical floor. This salon was hot.

The year was 1995. I had recently received my cosmetology license from Osborne School of Cosmetology after passing the state board of cosmetology exam. I had already been working at the salon for about six months. My time there was remarkable. Stephanie was the kind of salon owner who let you take the lead in the salon if you had an idea and could execute said idea properly. Because of this, I was able to start programs like the Toys for Kids Christmas Drive, which they kept going even after I left the salon.

This was a time when the local hip-hop radio station, 97.5, had Chris Lova Lova, aka Ludacris, as the radio personality, and Chaka Zula, Luda's manager at the time, as the promotions and radio personality at the station. La La Anthony, actress and Carmelo Anthony's ex-wife, was also an intern at the radio station while she was still a high school student. She then went on to continue her education at Howard. This time was also the era of Princess Ivory and Eboni Electra, all of whose hair I did while at Phawless Hair Design. I styled several other celebrities during that time too, such as Kandi Burruss and Tiny Harris from the multi-platinum singing group Xscape. My memories are so great from P.H.D. because I was young and ambitious. And now, 30 years later, the way I began in the beauty business—with skill, education, integrity, and that go-getting spirit—has opened the door to the résumé I carry today.

I've always believed in having a teachable spirit, and that belief led me to Spelman College as a Pauline E. Drake Scholar pursuing a Bachelor of Arts degree. Pauline E. Drake had a vision for nontraditional students to enter academia with the resources to balance financial and life obligations. Spelman was initiated with eleven students, primarily women and a few girls, and this program, in my eyes, was rooted in that same principle of access and opportunity.

The Pauline E. Drake program became my mentoring space, where I would earn my degree, be mentored, and mentor others. At the time, there was no real space for beauty as it related to hair within academia. Yet each year, awareness of the beauty industry and its relevance began to emerge.

During my junior year at Spelman, I opened a natural hair salon. There, I met my first contract hairstylist. She went on to graduate from Spelman, obtain her cosmetology license, and is now a successful, well-known interior decorator.

By combining mentorship with my love for beauty, I secured positions with companies like Dr. Miracles, Revlon, Clinique, Beautiful Textures, and Design Essentials. A time I remember fondly is being in Paris, teaching 3,000 women with natural hair from all over Europe—women who did not speak English. We had an interpreter to translate, but the energy needed no translation. It was incredible and reminded me of the importance of my role in the beauty industry.

Throughout my career I've opened three successful salons in Atlanta. At one point I had two locations at the same time. I also started a natural hair product line that is available at beauty supply stores, health food co-ops, and online. I then created a Natural Hair / Braiding Academy where I trained and certified several students into technical and business entrepreneurship of the beauty industry. I graced a magazine cover and had several hairstyles published in hair magazines. One of my dreams with hair was to see my work on the big screen by styling actress's hair. I am grateful that I was able to work with Ava DuVernay and Rosario Dawson on the *DMZ miniseries*. I worked with Ryan Coogler on *Black Panther: Wakanda Forever* creating the loc look for Lupita Nyong'o. I also styled Micheal B. Jordan. My goal was always to be the best at my craft, and that drive still yields me optimal opportunities. How you do one thing is surely how you do all things. And that is an African proverb I will never forget.

Nekesa's Tips

Your hair is your crown. Your hairstyle is a representation of your lifestyle and career. You are not your hair, however, a new hairstyle can renew your spirit, boost self-esteem, and confidence. Here are some tips to remember to help you wear your crown with confidence:

- Love yourself.
- Know your self-worth.
- Practice a fit lifestyle.
- Embrace your natural beauty.
- Rock your crown royally.

LET YOUR INNER RADIANCE SHINE

"I don't know if this style will look good on me; it looks good on her, but I don't know." In the twenty years that I have been taking care of clients and their hair, I have heard this response numerous times. It is quite a common sentiment shared amongst women, whether they are relaxed, cut, colored, or weaved. Clients see other clients, hair models, and celebrities, and love the styles they see, but when it comes to them trying it out on themselves, they're finicky. My remedy for this is to "let your inner goddess show." Trying a new hairstyle can be a daunting task. I always have to remind clients that it is just hair and that it is okay to have fun with it every now and then. Yet, I would never give a client a drastic change without having a consultation and being sure that that is exactly what the client wants, first.

When getting a new style, remember these tips:

- You are letting your inner goddess show; don't be afraid to try something new!
- Own your confidence through your poise and smile. Practice self-love through positive affirmations and daily habits.
- Know that your natural hair texture is your crown and that you should handle yourself accordingly. You are a queen and your hair is your crown.

Enhancing your life one strand at a time can apply to more than just your hair. It can apply to opening a new business, starting and raising a family, or beginning a health and wellness journey. There's no quick fix. If you want to open that business or go to school, it starts with enhancing your life one strand at a time. Let the world see your inner goddess shine through your outer appearance.

Nekesa's Tips

• Know that you are made perfect, as you are an imperfect image of God. You are naturally radiant and have a purpose that has been decided for you. All you have to do is walk in your essence.

• Adopt a health and wellness lifestyle of being active, thinking positively, and eating as close to nature as possible. Be free and honest in all things you do.

• Always educate yourself through reading, listening to all genres of music, and constantly learning. Take time to hang out in your local library, take a couple of hours to sit and read. Take notes and absorb all that is around you.

KNOW YOUR OWN HAIR TEXTURE

Many clients look online or see an advertisement and desire the same look that they are presented with. I always advise my clients that no matter how lovely the model's hair looks or how promising the hair company claims to be, you must know your *own* hair texture. You have to know what works for your hair texture, density, and length. Products used are not the end of this dilemma; they are simply an addition to the process.

There are several types of hair textures when it comes to natural hair care. There has been much discussion over the years about different hair textures, such as 4C, 3A, etc. However, many of these conversations aren't happening between true cosmetologists. These textures make sense in the full scope of breaking down natural hair and assisting in educating women about their hair, however, the hair texture is much more complex and vast than the typical 4A / 3B concept.

The Science & Structure of Hair

Natural hair is sensitive and the most outstanding feature of natural hair is its texture. The hair shaft consists of a medullary cortex and follicle. The looser the curl, the more the hair retains moisture and has the ability to grow. What happens in the looser curl patterns is that it is easier for the hair's natural oils to travel from the root to the tip. The curlier or wirier the hair is, the slower it takes for the oil to travel down the hair shaft to the ends. The natural hair oil usually stops midway down the shaft, causing dryness, breakage, and slow growth. The different textures are as follows:

- Curly 'S': this pattern refers to a natural wave formation in the hair strand that curves gently back and forth like the letter S.
- Coily 'Z': this pattern describes a hair strand that bends sharply in zig zag angles rather than forming rounded curls.
- Wavy 'Z': this pattern of hair is a texture that appears loosely and wavy at first glance, but contains zig zag bends within the strand.
- Straight curly: this pattern is straight at the root and curls towards the ends.

Fine hair is easily confused with a full, thick head of hair because of its texture and look. I have found that when clients have a thin coily 'Z' pattern or a coily 'S' pattern, their hair is very soft. Coils and rod sets work best for this hair pattern. The curly 'S' pattern hair is categorized as 3A, 3B, and 3C. This hair is more of a looser curl and can be categorized as fine, medium, or thick. These textures are great for wash-and-go styles, as well as two-strand twist-outs. The 'Z' pattern is categorized as 4B and 4C. The 'Z' pattern hair has a zig-zag pattern and varies from thin hair to thick hair. This hair texture is good for rod sets, coil sets, and braid sets.

There is a high chance that you have several textures on your head. Generally, my clients have thickness towards the crown of their head, while around the hairline in the front can be thinner, with a looser texture. The hairline closer to the nape of the neck could also be described as having a tighter texture.

The real reason certain styles look good on certain textures is because of the moisture balance in the hair. The process of hair is based on sulfur-rich proteins that the hair is composed of, and provides strength called keratin. Each strand of hair comes from a tiny tubular-shaped pocket in the skin called a follicle. The base of the follicle emerges from a tubular pocket where the hair emerges. The base of the follicle is called the papilla, which is a source of blood, oxygen, and new cells. The cells multiply in the papilla and become an individual strand of hair in three separate layers.

The first layer is the cuticle, which is the outermost layer. The cuticle's main job is to protect the two inner layers from the loss of moisture. Inside the cuticle is the cortex. It contains the pigment that provides the hair's color. The core of the hair shaft is called the medulla. The medulla contains a small core of cells that runs the length of the hair shaft.

Your scalp naturally produces sebum from the sebaceous glands. The sebum travels down the hair shaft. People with straight hair have to shampoo their hair often because the sebum easily travels down the hair shaft. With curlier, textured hair, the sebum has to work harder to go down the hair shaft due to the fact that it does not directly travel down. Depending on how loose or tight the curl is, the harder the sebum has to work to travel to the ends of hair.

Protective Style Options

Protective styles are natural hair options for those who are natural or transitioning to be natural. These styles are available to offer hair options that provide more longevity because there is typically hair added to provide that lasting power. Here is a short list of some protective style options:

- Two-strand twists - a hairstyle created by twisting two sections of hair around one another; can be combined with other styles such as afros, braids, etc.
- Serenity Twist - A signature style created by Nekesa that is a method similar to two strand twists; these are created with a kinky hair blend great as a protective style or loc start.

- Faux locs - artificial or false locs, imitation locs created by twisting or braiding the natural hair (with added extensions), then wrapping artificial hair around the original braid
- Diamond cut twists - a specific type of two strand twists; made with a 'diamond' part; thinner and lighter than two-strand twists
- Havana twists - variation of two-strand twists; larger twists that do not need specific parts, as they are done with curly extension hair meant to blend with natural hair
- Casamas - braids; generally thicker and longer than traditional box braids that are also done with three strands of hair; can be done with extensions
- Bush baby - a hairstyle inspired by Aborigines; a curly afro hairstyle
- Hair weaving - a style achieved when one's natural hair is braided, typically into a pattern; extensions are then sewn or glued on the client's preference; the extensions can be curled, straightened, cut and styled to the client's liking
- Crochet - a technique similar to hair weaving; instead of sewing or gluing the hair in, the hair is crocheted in using a regular crochet needle

These styles last from 8 to 12 weeks, depending on your preference. I do advise clients to have their protective style touched up within six weeks. This includes getting a shampoo, conditioning treatment, and getting the perimeter of the hairline retouched.

Hi Texture Hair Styles

Hi texture styles consist of hair in its natural state, then having the option of creating an additional hi-texture look. These looks are as follows:

- Twist set
- Rod set
- Braid set
- Coil set
- Finger coil set

These styles typically last 1 to 2 weeks. The maintenance of a textured set is simply a process of sleeping with a satin pillowcase, bonnet, or silk scarf nightly. In the morning, wake the curls up with a light scalp massage and a simple reshape of the curls.

WEAR YOUR HAIR LIKE YOU WEAR YOUR FAVORITE SHOES

The two things that I cannot live without are my custom crown and the shoes I use to walk in my destiny. I like to change my hair often, almost as much as I change my shoes. My suggestion to you for choosing a hairstyle is the same one I have about changing shoes: base it on how you feel. The beauty of natural hair is that it gives you the option of going from a short curly tapered set to a tapered diamond cut twist style in the span of a week or two. You can have a textured inverted bob crochet style to a cornrow style over to the side offering an instant facelift! So when choosing these styles, have fun! Experiment until you find your signature look. Enjoy the journey of customizing your crown as often as you like, just like you switch your shoes up to walk into your destiny.

It's wonderful to care for your natural hair at home, and I always educate my clients on how to maintain their hair between visits. However, just because your hair is natural doesn't mean you should avoid seeing a licensed professional. Your natural tresses deserve consistent, skilled care. When it comes to your crown, or even your shoes, this is not the place to cut corners. I was taught to invest in quality shoes because your feet are important extremities that require proper care through pedicures, massages, and reflexology. Your hair deserves that same level of attention. So invest in finding, and staying with, a good beautician. At the same time, don't allow just anyone to touch your hair. It's important to choose someone who is not only knowledgeable about natural hair care, but also caring, professional, uplifting, honest, and full of integrity. The following companies are brands I've observed and trust, aligned with strong business values and a genuine commitment to caring for their clients and customers.

Nekesa's Top Five: Hair Companies, Salons Etc.

Natural Hair Salons

- Khamit Kinks (NYC)
- The Sunrisa (Paris)
- Mahogany Revolution (LA)
- Nekesa's Natural Radiance (ATL)
- Twists, Braids, Curls (Connecticut)

Trusted Product Companies

- Nekesa's Naturals
- Pattern Beauty
- Design Essential
- Avalon
- Aveda

Natural Hair Extension Companies

- Curlkalon
- Heat free curls
- Afro Niva
- Top Tier
- Lux Hair Lugo

EPILOGUE

If you have made it to this final page, then you have walked with me from the little girl fascinated by texture and transformation, to the woman who understands that hair has always been far more than beauty. It is herstory, resistance, artistry, and science.

When I first picked up a comb, I did not yet know that I was stepping into an archive. I did not know that every scalp I touched carried chemistry, culture, and a story. Textured hair is electric. It defies gravity. It bends without breaking. It spirals toward the sun. It is stem and poetry at the same time. And caring for it requires both knowledge and reverence.

Enhancing your life one strand at a time was never just about styling. It became about studying. Researching. Teaching. Preserving. It became about understanding the natural molecular integrity of the hair fiber while honoring the cultural integrity of the women who wear it.

My growth expanded when I stepped into the role of oral historian at Spelman College, not just as a beauty professional, but as a scholar of our lived beauty experiences. In the classrooms and corridors shaped by Black intellectual legacy, I began documenting the stories of cosmetic chemists, innovators, and beauty pioneers. I witnessed firsthand how science and story intersect, how formulation labs and salon chairs are connected by the same pursuit: advancement.

Beauty is not surface. It is STEM. It is research. It is entrepreneurship. It is community knowledge that passed down the practice of beauty long before institutions recognized it as expertise.

Personally, I have grown in ways the younger version of me could not have imagined. I have learned to slow down without shrinking. I have learned that discipline is love in action. I have learned that wellness is not indulgence, it is infrastructure. And I have learned that legacy is not built loudly, but intentionally.

There were seasons of stretching, seasons of reinvention, and seasons where I had to confront my own doubts and recalibrate my pace, but every layer added dimension. Every pivot added wisdom and every chapter added depth.

Growth, like textured hair, is layered. It expands. It coils back. It moves in patterns you may not immediately understand but it is always forming.

Today, I stand as a beauty professional, educator, scholar, entrepreneur, and cultural archivist, not because I chased titles, but because I committed to evolution. Enhancement is not about appearance. It is about alignment. It is about stewardship of your gifts. It is about honoring your strands and the stories woven within them.

If this book has offered anything, I hope it has offered you perspective. That your texture is not something to tame, but something to study. Not something to hide, but something to radiantly electrify the room. Care for your strands. Protect your peace. Build your legacy.

With intention and radiance,

Nekesa Namosunge J. Smith

PHOTO ALBUM

1

1- My first school picture; 2nd grade 1982
at St. Peters Catholic private school

My 2nd grade class in 1982

2

My Salt-N-Pepa hip-hop inspired bob
for my 9th grade coordination ball

3

4

Family Pics 1989. Hair by me - microbraids on myself, hairstyling on mom, pontoons bangs on my sister

5

Dad and I, 16 years-old, with a hip hop inspired sew in

6

Tavia and I in Atlanta Hairstyle Magazine, 1995

7

Young, gifted, and Black in Hotlanta

8

Black Sophisticates Hair Magazine feature with my friend and hairmodel, Makebia J.

9

I was surprised at being featured on the cover of Real Styles magazine in 1996

10

Hype Hair Magazine flat twist feature, 1996

11

Speaking at my graduation for Cosmetology School

12

Beautifully Driven to the Hair Capital,
at one of the many class events I produced and taught

13

Radiant Beauty living free with cornrows by the sea

The crown is yours, you just need to make the decision to wear it. This is 13 years of Serenity Locs growth. 14

Beautifully driven to the hair capital to see and learn from icons who I have admired like Charles Gregory. Fast forward to this pic when we worked on the Ava DuVernay series DMZ. This was days before COVID-19. The production was shut down, as well as my salon in Atlanta. It was also Charles's birthday; he passed away a month later 15

16

Know, learn, and love your hair texture

17

Teaching texture at Design Essentials Labs

18

Teaching at Taliah Wahjid Natural Hair Show

19

Radiant beauties and I. All styles done by me

20

Teaching Natural Hair Texture with students at a Natural Hair Academy, 2014

21

Standing outside Rosario Dawson's trailer

22

23

24

Styling Lupita Nyongo's hair for Black Panther: Wakanda Forever

25

On set with Rosario Dawson, 2022

26

Rocking my Nekesa's Natural Radiance (NNR) jacket

27

Styled a radiant beauty for her wedding day, 2025

28

Crowned Radiant Beauty, Wedding Bliss, 2025

29

Nekesa's Natural Radiance Hair Nourisher. Est.1999

30

Doing what I love, custom crowning a radiant beauty for her wedding.

31

31 - And with these hands

Love is in the hair.

NATURAL HAIR GLOSSARY

2nd Day Hair - natural hair that still looks good after wearing the same style for a second day

3A/3B/3C - classification numbers for natural hair. This hair type has a loose curl pattern.

4A/4B/4C - classification number for natural afro textured hair

Apple Cider Vinegar (ACV) - used as a final rinse after shampooing the hair, and sometimes used before conditioning to seal the cuticle

Afro - naturally curly/kinky hair styled in a round shape, or is naturally round shape when loose

AO / Aubrey Organics - hair care product line that contains natural and organic ingredients

APL / Arm Pit Length - a term used to describe the growth of your hair when it has reached your armpit

Argan Oil - a vitamin E-rich oil derived from Morocco that contains essential fatty acids and is used to moisturize the hair. Also known as Moroccan Oil

BAA / Big Ass Afro - an afro that is very large in size because the naturally curly/kinky hair is very long

Baggy - method used to help reduce breakage and dryness by sleeping with a plastic cap on and your hair to help keep it moisturized. This is normally done after some type of moisturizer has been applied to the hair and the ends of the hair sealed with oil

Bantu Knot - style created when the hair is sectioned off and twisted into two strand twists and then twisted around in a circle/ knot

Bantu Knot Out - styling wet or damp hair into bantu knots, allowing it to dry and unraveling all of them once they are dry

BC / Big Chop - the process of cutting chemically treated (relaxed) hair completely off to leave only afro textured/natural textured hair

BKT / Brazilian Keratin Treatment - hair straightening treatment that lasts temporarily and sometimes includes the use of formaldehyde

BNC / Braid n Curl - braiding wet or damp hair and curling the ends with rollers or curling rods. Once the hair is dry, the rollers and braids are taken out to reveal wavy hair with curly ends

Braidlocs - the process of locing hair (sometimes without doing the big chop) by braiding it into small braids and maintaining it by latching or palm rolling the new growth

Braid Out - hairstyle achieved by braiding damp or moist hair and unraveling it once it is dry so the hair can achieve more defined curls/waves

BSL / Bra Strap Length - term used to describe the growth of your hair when it has reached the area down your back where your bra strap is located

BSS / Beauty Supply Store - A retail store with various hair products, accessories, and cosmetics.

Buds (Budding) - term used to describe the beginning stages of locs

CBL / Collar Bone Length - term used to describe the growth of your hair when it has reached your collar bone

Co-wash - washing hair with conditioner only, to keep the hair soft and manageable, since washing black hair with shampoo often can be drying to the hair

Coils - styling technique created by using a rattail comb to twist small sections of the hair into coils. This hairstyle is normally worn by women with shorter length hair

Cones (Silicones) - ingredients in some hair care products that help to condition the hair and give it some shine

Cornrow - braiding the hair close to the scalp in a continuous row

Creamy Crack - phrase used to describe hair relaxers because of the tendency for it to be hard to stop the relaxing process to go back natural

Denman - this company manufactures a hairbrush used by a number of women with natural hair

Detangler - conditioning product that helps to prevent/comb through tangles

Detangling - the process of using a detangler or leave-in conditioner to comb through the hair with more ease

DIY / Do It Yourself -referring to the activity of doing you hairstyle or haircare for yourself.

DT (Deep Treatment) / DC (Deep Conditioning) - moisturizing treatment that uses heat to help penetrate the hair to add moisture to the hair and make the hair soft and more manageable

Dusting - trimming very little off the ends of the hair. The amount of hair trimmed is minimal and tends to look like dust on the floor once cut off

EO / Essential Oils - natural oils (Rosemary, Sweet Orange, Peppermint, Lemon, Avocado oil, etc) that gives hair shine and promotes healthy hair

EVCO / Extra Virgin Coconut Oil - natural conditioner that gives the hair shine and makes it soft

Flat Twist - twisting the hair flat to the head, similar to braiding but instead of using three strands of hair, two strands (such as in two-strand twists) are used and a braiding technique using those two pieces are applied

Fluff - finger combing the hair to create volume

FSG / Flax Seed Gel - flax seed based styling gel that is usually homemade, but some companies such as Aveda, makes a flax seed styling gel

Henna - a plant used as a hair dye

Hand in Hair (HIH) / Hair in Fro (HIF) - terms used for playing in your hair/fro

JBCO / Jamaican Black Castor Oil - type of castor oil made in Jamaica for use on the hair

KCCC / Kinky Curly Custard - styling gel product that contains natural ingredients

Latch Hooking - loc maintenance method to "hook" the new growth into the existing locs

MBL / Mid Back Length - term used for when the hair grows and reaches the middle of your back in length

Nappyversary / Nappy Anniversary - the anniversary of the day when all chemically (relaxed) treated hair is cut off and the hair is worn fully natural

No-Poo - the process of using something other than shampoo to wash your hair. In most cases, conditioner is used

ORS / Organic Root Stimulator - hair care product line with herbal ingredients

Palm Rolling - method for maintaining traditional locs that involves placing individual locs between the palms and rubbing it back and forth to tighten

Pineapple-ing - placing the hair in a high ponytail on top of the head in order to maintain curl or waves for a twist out or other style, and taking it down for a second day

Pixies - small individual braids (with or without weave) that are also known as box braids. If weave is used, the ends are sealed with heat and curled

Plopping - drying hair (without manipulating it) by wrapping in a towel or other cotton material as a way to dry the hair quickly and keep curls defined

Pre-Poo - saturating the hair with a deep conditioner, damage repair treatment, or oils for longer than 15 minutes before shampooing the hair

Protective Style - hairstyle that keeps your ends protected to minimize breakage and split ends. This also includes refraining from using heat on the hair and avoiding everyday styling, combing, and brushing. Some examples are twists left in for long stretches of time that are worn tucked in, weaves, wigs, buns, and braided hairstyles

Regimen - your daily or weekly hair styling routine

S&Ds / Search and Destroy - checking the hair for knots and split ends and trimming them off

Sealing - applying oil or shea butter (or another butter of choice) to the ends of the hair after using a water based moisturizer to "seal the ends" and retain moisture

Shingling - combing gel, conditioner, or a pomade to spread it from roots to ends, which allows the hair to stretch and define curls

SL / Sisterlocks - very small locs that are created using a specialized tool to loc the hair without gels, pomades, or waxes

Slip - the feel (how slippery) of a conditioner, detangler, or gel on hair

TNC / Twist n Curl - two strand twisting dry, wet or damp hair and using rollers on the ends of the hair, drying the hair with the use of a hair dryer or allowing it to dry overnight and once dry, taking out rollers and unraveling the twists

ACKNOWLEDGEMENTS

To my husband, children, and family: thank you so much for all your support, love, and patience during this journey. Without you, I would not be where I am today. From assisting me in editing, encouraging me to power forward, traveling state to state and even internationally, to make this thing happen! Thanks for hosting product parties at your house, referring coworkers, and even babysitting when I was "making it happen." Words can't express my love for you all.

Thanks and much love to Twin Chelly, Ro, Mom LeWanda, Linda Jackson, Naomi Knox, Sharyn Grant, and Rhonda Watts.

Thanks to my NNR Hair and Loft family, aka clients, who are a part of one of my dreams of being an influential beauty professional. To my Spelman sisterhood: thanks to all of you who inspire me and hold me up daily to be the change I want to see. Your stories, advice, and actions are priceless, and I am forever grateful. Thanks to my Phawless Hair Design family. Thank you to my friends for all of your support, from helping me produce my first hair show at the age of 19 at the Melebus Club in New Haven, Connecticut to the present shows and seminars. Thanks for being my muse and allowing me to use your hair as my canvas, ALWAYS.

To all of the visitors of the salon and website: thanks for all your positive comments and insights.

Xo, Nekesa

ABOUT THE AUTHOR

Nekesa "Namosunge" J. Smith is a Spelman College graduate and a licensed cosmetology professional with over 20 years of experience. She is an expert and international educator on natural hair. In 1999, Nekesa's love for hair led her to develop her own natural hair care line, Nekesa's Natural Radiance Beauty Company. While the line started with the 3-N-1 Deep Moisturizer, Nekesa has since added 10 other natural, alcohol-free products to the NNRBC line, while also offering salon services and monthly classes. In 2010, she was blessed to open a second salon in Atlanta, GA where her vision of providing a creative space where women could come to learn about and embrace their natural hair texture came to life. In 2016, Nekesa's love for hair care and women's empowerment birthed a new baby and labor of love, her first book, Enhancing Your Life One Strand at a Time, a personal memoir and professional guide to enhancing your life one strand at a time. That same year, she also began "Doing It Her Way University," a class dedicated to empowering women to invest in themselves while teaching them how to develop their passions and crafts into a profitable business. Today, Nekesa resides in Atlanta, Georgia, with her husband and two children, promoting the NNRBC brand and encouraging and inspiring new ways to keep women around the world radiant.

Connect With the Author:

www.nekesanaturals.myshopify.com

IG: @nekesanaturals_haircare

www.ingramcontent.com/pod-product-compliance
Ingram Content Group UK Ltd.
Pitfield, Milton Keynes, MK11 3LW, UK
UKRC031052310726
14090UKWH00028B/476

* 9 7 8 1 9 7 2 2 3 5 0 0 3 *

9 781972 235003